Mel Bay Presents

Hints and Tips For Advanced Ukulele Players

By H. M. "Heeday" Kimura

2 3 4 5 6 7 8 9 0

Visit us on the Web at www.melbay.com — E-mail us at email@melbay.com

Table of Contents

Matchcover Strumming E Picking

To get a unique "flap" strumming sound, get a book match cover and use one corner like a pick (Fig. 3).

Caution! If you overdo this or if you use too stiff a match cover for this, you may mar the surface of your uke sound box. If you intend to use this or other types of picks (See also blurb on "Mandolin Effect"), it may be wise to install a plastic guard glued to your uke under the sound hole as shown in Fig. 4. Some players put guards both above and below the sound hole; however, be aware that placement of guards can alter the quality of your uke tone quality.

When doing the match cover strum, just skim over the strings very lightly. For melody playing, use the banjo style or multiple string technique wherein you include the melody while playing all four strings. The "single string picking" using the soft match cover does not give you much volume. Try combining this effect with the match-box "maracas" effect.

TYPICAL MATCHCOVER

Fig. 1

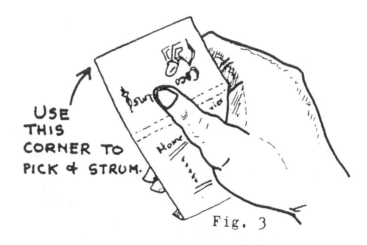

USE THIS CORNER TO PICK & STRUM.

Fig. 3

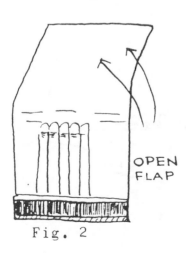

OPEN FLAP

Fig. 2

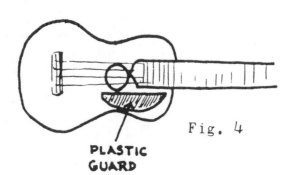

Fig. 4

PLASTIC GUARD

Curved Botton Ukes

For those who intend to have a craftsman make that ideal ukulele, one suggestion is to have the bottom curved acoustically. You have probably seen guitars with the curved bottom.

Consider that ukuleles are smaller than guitars and do not have the acoustical volume of guitars. I mention this because there are those who say that the curved bottom guitars are no better than the flat bottom ones, especially if those flat-bottoms are of concert quality. Yet, fretted instrument craftsmen have told me that no matter how good an instrument maker is, only one out of roughly seven instruments can be classified as concert quality. If this is true, the principle holds **true** for ukes also. Adding a curved bottom can enhance even the non-concert quality instrument.

Problem is that not many manufacturers make curved bottoms because of the additional skills and tooling involved. But if you're in the market for a custom-made uke, ask your craftsman about a rounded bottom uke. The curved back concert ukulele maker whom I bought the uke from passed away and there went my chance to have a more specifically custom made uke from him. The one I had bought from him was a ready-made model.

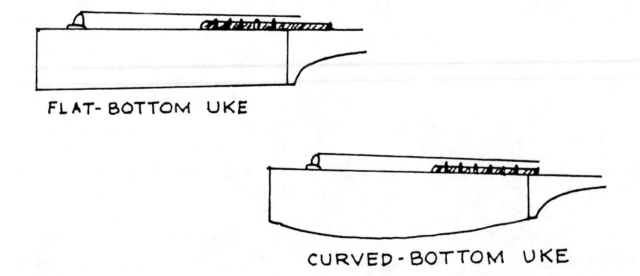

FLAT-BOTTOM UKE

CURVED-BOTTOM UKE

Percussion Ukulele

You can use the ukulele as a percussion strumming instrument and a picking device by using an unsharpened pencil that has a rubber eraser tip. To strum, you merely hold the uke in the customary position and strike the flat sides of the pencil against all four strings in time to your singing, whistling, humming, etc. You can even pick out melodies on single strings with this method, although some may find it a bit awkward. If you like this position, here's how you would place the pencil to strike the strings.

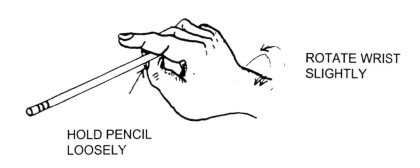

ROTATE WRIST
SLIGHTLY

HOLD PENCIL
LOOSELY

Perhaps a slightly more comfortable position would be to hold the uke in the customary position with your left hand as holding chords, then letting the sound box slide down to your lap so that the uke is now held upright like a bass fiddle. Of course, you are in a seated position. Then you simply "strum" or "pick" the strings as above. Your pencil-holding position will naturally have to be modified to facilitate the percussion. Here is a suggested way, but you can concoct your own.

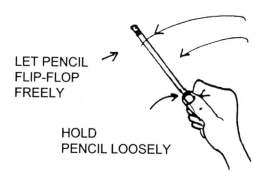

LET PENCIL
FLIP-FLOP
FREELY

HOLD
PENCIL LOOSELY

Your imagination knows no bounds so try to figure out other ways in which you can create new and novel ways to use a pencil, or for that matter any other implement to add enjoyment to your uke playing!

Snare Drum Effect

When playing marches like "Marines Hymn", "Caissons Go Rolling", "Stars And Strips Forever", etc., you can create the snare drum effect by deadening all four strings and strumming across all four in usual strumming fashion. You can deaden the strings merely by holding them very lightly with all four fingers of the left hand. A simple intro to, say, "Marines Hymn" would be the rhythm "ta-tum, ta-tum, ta-tum-tum-tum" strummed over the "dead" strings about three or four times and then immediately picking the melody.

Mandolin Effect

You can create a strong mandolin effect on your uke with a regular single-string or multiple-strings tremolo with your fingers. By using a regular guitar plastic pick, you can get a "cleaner" and richer tone on the tremolo because of the relative stiffness-yet-flexible-nature of the pick. This effect, however, is not recommended unless you have a non-scuff type plastic or wooden guard installed on your uke.

Many years ago, I became so intrigued with the brilliance of the tremolo when done with a stiff pick, that I used it on my favorite Martin 16-fretter soprano uke with disastrous results! Before I knew it, the top veneer had worn away so badly that in time a hole emerged. I had a friend glue on a plastic guard to cover the hole, but the sound has never been the same. You may want to at least experiment, but don't go hog wild lest you end up with a "puka" uke (Hawaiian pidgin for holy [not religious-wise] ukulele).

Bellows Effect

To get a bellowing sound from your uke, blow into the sound hole of your instrument at a slight angle. You have to experiment with several angles to get the most resonant spot.

How To Do The "Trill"

The "trill" is a rapid pressing and releasing of a string. Let's try a sample:

1. Put your index finger on the first fret of the bottom string.
2. Pluck the string and immediately strike the same string at the 3rd fret with your left ring finger (hammering motion) in a rapid piston-like action, alternately striking and releasing the ring finger.

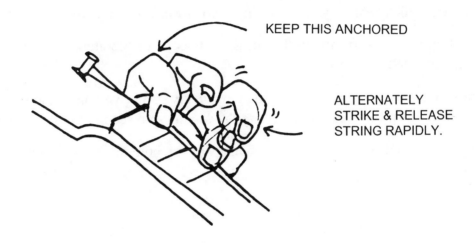

KEEP THIS ANCHORED

ALTERNATELY
STRIKE & RELEASE
STRING RAPIDLY.

A good exercise to "educate" your fingers to the trill is to do the key of "C" scale. It will actually be a hammering drill for your fingers. Press the strings shown here and practice a rapid press, release, press (which will evolve into the hammer or piston-like action).

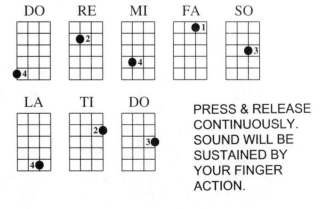

PRESS & RELEASE
CONTINUOUSLY.
SOUND WILL BE
SUSTAINED BY
YOUR FINGER
ACTION.

How To Do The "Slide"

The "slide" will add a "polished" sound to your uke solos. As the name implies, the " slide" is done by sliding any finger from one fret to another.

Follow these steps:

1. Place your little finger on the bottom string at the 10th fret.

2. Pick the string. Allowing only a split second for the string to be plucked at the 10th fret fingered position, immediately slide your little finger downward (toward fret one) to fret 7.

   Be sure to press down firmly on the string even as you slide along it. This makes for a "cleaner" sound, not muffled.

   At first you may have a tendency to slide too quickly. After you have done it a few times, slide a bit more leisurely as if to give each fret along the way its split second to "sound off".

3. When you can do it comfortably, do the same slide by holding the "C" chord.

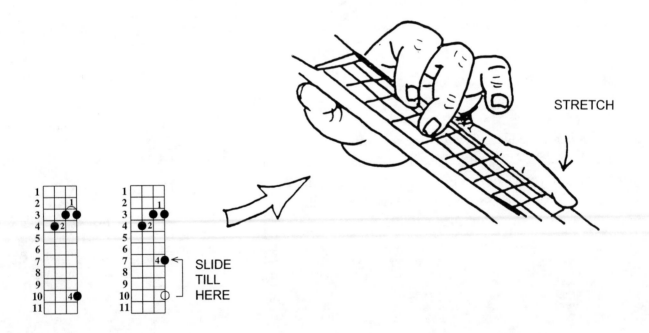

SLIDE
TILL
HERE

STRETCH

How To Do The "Wa-Wa" Effect

To play the "wa-wa" or "wavering effect" on your uke, place the heel of your right (or picking) hand squarely over all four strings at the raised crosspiece of the ukulele bridge located on the sound box. Place the palm heel on the raised strings slightly behind the portion where the strings leave the cross piece. If your palm pads follow the strings too much beyond the crosspiece and toward the sound hole, the strings will be too muffled.

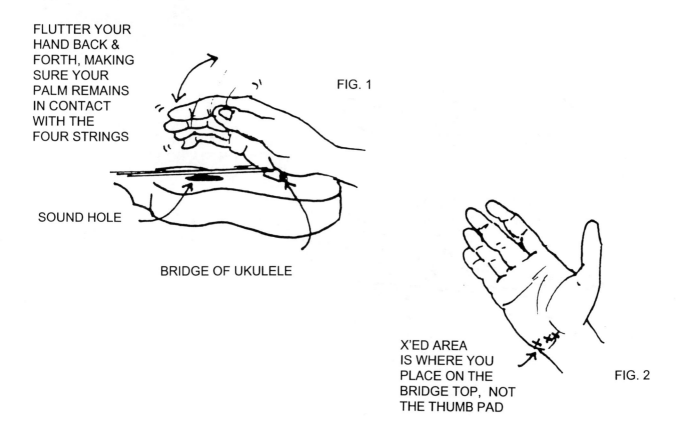

FLUTTER YOUR HAND BACK & FORTH, MAKING SURE YOUR PALM REMAINS IN CONTACT WITH THE FOUR STRINGS

FIG. 1

SOUND HOLE

BRIDGE OF UKULELE

X'ED AREA IS WHERE YOU PLACE ON THE BRIDGE TOP, NOT THE THUMB PAD

FIG. 2

When placing your palm heel, use the small finger side, not the thumb base pad. Then you'll be able to strum more freely. To do the "wa-wa" effect, move or "flutter your fingers in the direction shown by the arrows. This will cause the x'ed pad area (see fig. 2) to alternately release and exert pressure on the strings, causing the "wa-wa" effect. You can add a bit of showmanship by fluttering the fingers over the sound hole!

How To Play The "Chimes"

To make your uke sound like highly pitched chimes, start at the 12th fret, bottom string ("A" string) extend your little finger upward with palms open and contact the tip bottom of the finger very lightly on the "A" string. Pluck the "A" string with your right thumb and quickly release your left little finger from the "A" string.   If your timing is correct, you will hear the chime effect clearly. If not, you will hear either the regular "A" string pitch or a mere pluck of the string deadened by your little finger holding the string too long.

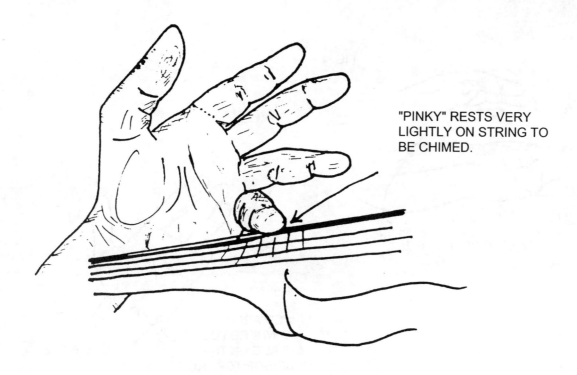

"PINKY" RESTS VERY LIGHTLY ON STRING TO BE CHIMED.

When you can "chime" the bottom string, work on the next string ("C" string). When successful, do the other strings at the 12th fret in turn. This effect is especially pleasing when playing Hawaiian slack key music (although you'll have to retune for slack key).

To retune for slack key, the sequence of strings from top to bottom is G, C, E, and G. If you want to experiment with the chimes, use all four strings (one at a time, of course, to play the military bugle calls like "Taps" at the 12th fret.

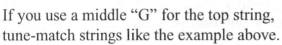

G'C E G'

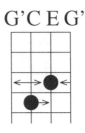

Low
G C E G'

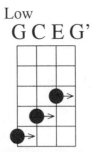

If you use a middle "G" for the top string, tune-match strings like the example above.

If you use a low top "G", follow this next example.

The 12th fret is the easiest spot on the fingerboard to do chimes. Once you develop the knack at the 12th fret, practice also at the 5th, 7th, and 10th frets. When you can pluck clear bell-tone chimes on the strings at those frets, you should have little trouble with other frets.

Aside from bugle calls you can use the chime effect as an intro to a song that has to do with bells, chimes, Christmas, etc.

Playing Behind The Head

If it's showmanship you're after, this is one of the best antics.

Hold the uke firmly but not rigidly against the neck muscles behind your head. Your arms and shoulders must especially be relaxed since you will be playing in a very awkward position. If you feel a bit "top heavy", that means you have too much tension in the shoulders.

If you can play fairly well from the regular sitting and standing positions, this technique shouldn't be too hard for you to master. Allow many sessions of practice before attempting public performances, however!

Start with very simple songs as you will be at a slight handicap in this back-of-head position.

How To Do The "Bend"

If you would like to add a touch of country-western or blues flavor to your melody playing, the "bend" is an excellent technique to work in.

Let's use the second string from the bottom ("E" string).

1. Hold the "E" string at the third fret with your left ring finger (assuming you are right-handed).

2. Pluck the string with your right thumb at the same instant the string is plucked. The left ring finger still holding down the string pushes it upward very slightly. You will hear the originally plucked pitch waver upward. Quickly return the string to its original position and you will hear the pitch you started off with. This is called the "Bend". You may have to do it a few times to get the knack.

3. Novelty effects like this would be of little value if you couldn't apply them to your own uke arrangements. The following exercise will help you to apply the bend.

Let's say that your song has an ending like this (a currently popular song):

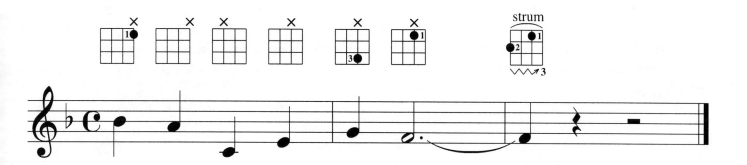

Play this several times until you memorize the melody. Then try the improvised version with the bend worked in.

How To Do The "Bend" (Continued)

Play this very slowly a first, then pick up speed only slightly as you master it. Played too fast, this technique loses its "color" and effectiveness.

Remember to "bend" the two consecutive "G" notes. Don't exceed one beat for each "G" note bend.

A variation is to do one long bend for the two beats. This is especially easy to do in the Key of F. Use the left ring finger.

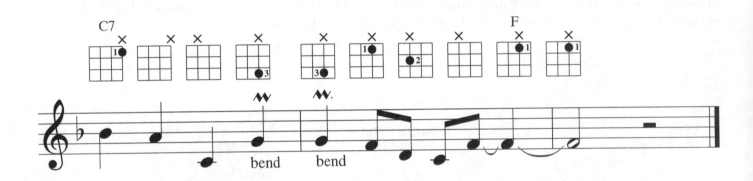

Thumb Picking

Advanced ukers are more and more resorting to the use of the thumb picking technique for solo playing.

Readers who wish to experiment with this technique should shape their thumbnails into a "pick" as shown. Try out different shapes and picking styles. Some pickers prefer the long pointed nails while others use a shorter version. Your Editor prefers the slightly shorter nail skewed left since he uses a "bent-thumb" angle. Many thumbnail pickers keep their thumbs extended while picking, while still others prefer lengths somewhere in between.

POINTED  BALANCED  SKEWED LEFT

More On Thumb Picking

Those who pick with the thumb need to be aware of two basic features. One is the use of the fleshy part of the thumbtip to get a muffled effect and the nail tip technique for a brighter clearer sound.

To experiment, use any one of the two middle strings. Imagine you are trying to rub the string against the fingerboard with your thumb (fleshy broad part).

Start with a slow "down-up" stroke, being careful not to hit the neighboring strings. Press down firmly on the string as you do this, but make sure the string can be sounded. Notice the muffled effect? This is the technique you can use for any staccatto or "horse-gallop" effect.

Now do the same thing using your nail tip technique and notice the difference as compared to the fleshy style. Notice the much cleaner and louder sound when you use the nail?

For the thumbnail-tip style, be sure to bend your thumbnail joint perpendicular to the strings.

Practice running your scales with these two styles every chance you get. You can vary your arrangements by picking the melody with the nail tip and strumming with the flesh tip technique, vice-versa.

* *

Tremolo Techniques

There are several tremolo techniques that can add varied sounds to your arrangements.

1. Single-string technique using any of the three fingers and the thumb.

2. Two-string tremolo techniques using any two fingers or thumb and any other finger.

3. Three-string tremolo using the thumb and two other fingers or three fingers (index, middle, and ring fingers)

4. Four-string tremolo using index alone, thumb alone, or two fingers (index and middle) alone

(continued on next page)

I. Single-String Tremolo. You can use either the index finger as shown here or the thumb nail. If you're doing single string without holding chords, be extra careful not to hit the other strings. The beauty of the single string tremolo would be lost if you allowed an accidental "blonk" sound from another string.

A variation to this single string technique is to brace your little finger to the sound box to give you a firmer base to do single string tremolo.

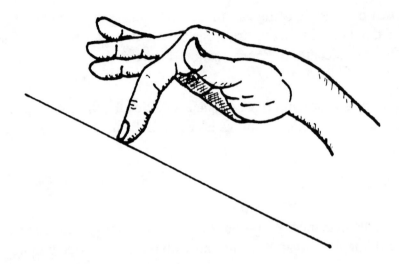

II. Two strings tremolo can be played with the thumbnail and index finger in combination. Another way is to use your index and middle fingers as shown in the illustration below.

On the single string technique, you can pretty much push your finger almost flush with the wooden surface, but with the two string technique, you'll have to "skim" the strings a little more than in the single-string because the fingernails tend to snag a little easier. Try several degrees of pressures to find your best method.

As in the single-string style, you may want to brace your little finger against the uke to give you more leverage on the rapid up-and-down moves of the tremolo.

USE TWO
NEIGHBOR STRINGS
WHEN USING INDEX-
MIDDLE FINGERS. USE
THUMB-INDEX FOR
SEPARATED.

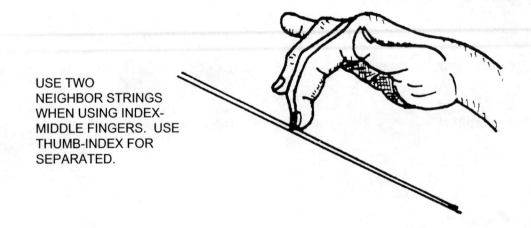

(Continued on next page)

The Three-Strings Tremolo

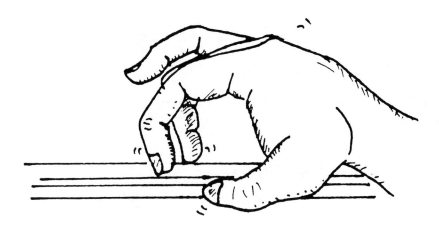

For the Three-Strings Tremolo, use the thumb and neighboring fingers. The index and middle fingers are the easiest to manipulate in conjunction with the thumb, but the ring finger can be worked in, especially where the strings are not right next to each other. For example, the thumb can tremolo the top string while the index tremolos the third string from the bottom and the ring finger works on the bottom string.

The single, double, and three-strings tremolos require a certain degree of practice since the volume will not be as loud as the four-string tremolo. Also the tendency for "snags" can create some problems because you are dealing with more than one finger. However, with a little bit of practice the knack should come rather easily, especially if you have done tremolos before.

The Four Strings Tremolo

This is the most dramatic of all the tremolos as you can vary from very loud to very soft. Run your index finger over all four strings especially when the melody is on the bottom string. With a bit of practice you can move in and out of single string tremolo as the melody moves to the inner strings. The wrist must be loose to effect the best tremolo. Practice high speed tremolo after you are able to do the basic four--strings tremolo smoothly.

"Coloring" Your Hawaiian Vamp

Excerpted From Ukefellows Newsletter
by Heeday

In my "Ukulele By 'Ear', Hawaiian Style" book, the "Hawaiian Vamp" was introduced in the song "U. S. E. D." a hula ditty with many stanzas.

The value of learning the Vamp is not only for learning the particular cultural musical style, but also for its applications to other songs.

For the beginner, the basic "D7-G7-C" Vamp in the Key of "C" can be used in many simple three chord songs. Once the vamp in the Key of "C" is mastered, the novice can move into other keys by consulting the transposition chart in the "ear" book.

To refresh your memory and to clarify what we mean by a Hawaiian Vamp, it's a "package" or "set" of three chords in definite sequence used as sort of a break at the end of each hula stanza.

The pattern is known as 117, V7, and I to jazz musicians. The Roman numerals tell you which note of a given scale you use to determine the progression. For example, if we are talking about the Key of "C" scale, they are C-D-E-F-G-A-B-C. The Roman numeral I in this key would naturally be "C" since it is the first note of the scale. Roman numeral II in the Key of C scale would be "D". Add the "7" and you end up with "D7". Roman numeral V in the Key of C scale is the fifth note of that scale--or "G". Again add the "7" and you end up with "G".

(If this is old hat to you, please bear with me as we have some "ear" players within our midst.)

I'll take you through the basics of the Hawaiian Vamp in the Key of "C" and then on to some intermediate level ad libs or variations that will be fun.

Let's play the basic Hawaiian Vamp in the Key of "C" first. Strum through it as patterned--four beats for the last chord of the stanza, two beats each for the D7 and G7 chords, and finally four beats for the "C" or "root" chord.

"Coloring" Your Hawaiian Vamp (Continued)

The slant marks represent one beat each. The broken arrows show you the timing or movement of your foot as illustrated in the examples below.

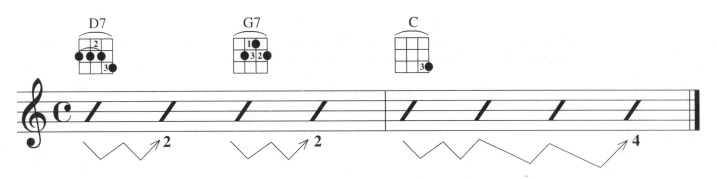

FOOT TIMING:

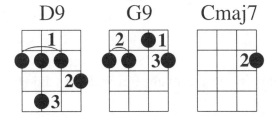 ETC.

Strum the above chords in your usual basic downstrum or up-and-down strum for the first few times.

To accustom your ear to jazz accompaniment, use only your thumb (fleshy tip and not the nail) in a downstrum only. It may sound a bit muffled at first but get used to the "flavor" of that sound. It will make your strumming sound a bit more sophisticated and take you a step into "blues" type chording.

Now, after you get the mood of that thumb sound, change the 7th Chords to 9th Chords. In other words, use D9 instead of D7 and G9 instead of G7. Also for the C chord, substitute the C major 7th chord.

As an aside for those new into this type of chording, some of these "color" chords may sound "foreign" or "wrong" to your ears.

The chords are "blues" type chords and until you get accustomed to them, you may remain on a "plateau" and be "hog-tied" to only basic chords. Keep on working on your "hearing"--no matter how difficult at first--so that you can "sense" the basic "D7-G7-C" sound within the new "D9-G9-Cmaj7" sequence.

On the C major 7th chord, be sure to sound out all four strings, especially the "C" string (third string from the bottom) which is the "root" or the indicator of what key you are strumming in.

When you have practiced enough to "hear" the changes, use the higher inversions of the same chords.

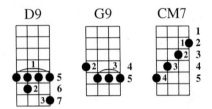

Then use the same dominant 9th chords that you have been using but this time use the C major 6th chord instead of the C major 7th chord. I have listed the more commonly used C6 (another way of saying "C major 6th") chords here. Use them one at a time with the D9-G9-C sequence.

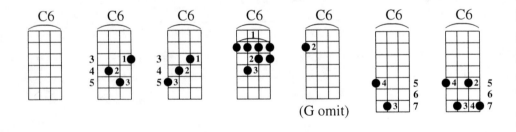

(G omit)

In other words, use any one of these C6 chords in place of the basic C chord.

These are variations that you can use interchangeably.

For advanced players who can "hear" the basic chord sounds in the dominant 9th and the Major 6th and 7th chords, let's move into what is known as substitute chords.

By selecting two notes from a 7th chord and adding two "color" notes from another chord, we can come out with interesting alterations. One formula you can use is to take the flatted 5th of the original 7th chord and use that as a substitute dominant 7th.

We can use a D♭7 chord in place of a G7 chord and an A♭7 in place of the D7 chord.

How did I figure this? Well, if we are looking for a substitute jazz chord, for the G7 chord, we go back to the Key of "G" scale (G-A-B-C-D-E-F♯-G). You will notice that the fifth note in that sequence is the "D" note. The substitute formula calls for flatting the 5th and using the dominant 7th of that step, resulting in "D♭".

To substitute the D7 chord, we use the Key of "D" scale (namely, D-E-F♯-G-A-B-C♯-D). If we take the fifth note in the sequence and flat it, we get "A♭". Hope this clarifies any cobwebs.

So let's try our new set of chords on the Hawaiian Vamp.

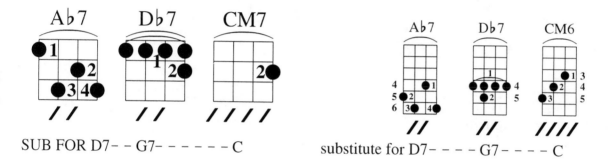

SUB FOR D7- - G7- - - - - -C   substitute for D7- - - - G7- - - - C

When your ears can "hear" these chords properly, move into the dominant 9th forms of the A♭7 and D♭7. Use either C major 7th or C major 6th to end.

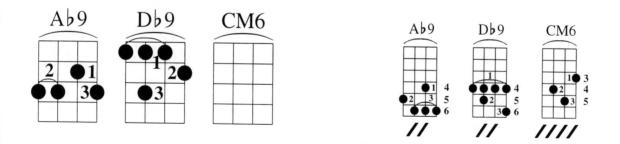

Advanced Variation. If you understand and have practiced "step-by-step" so far, you can now move into an experiment in making a chord change for every beat in the Hawaiian Vamp.

Remember, we are still using the pattern from the basic D7-G7-C arrangement.

In advanced chord substitution, there is often the attempt to get away from the monotony of using the same chord for more than a few beats. The extreme would be to change chords for every beat. However, caution is advised here in that too much overplay on substitution can take away the spirit of a song. Certain songs just don't sound right when too many jazz type chords are inserted.

Let's try to vary the C chord and its variations while we work in a chord per beat in the Hawaiian Vamp. For the last four beats of the Vamp, use in sequence (one beat each) the C, C major 7, C major 6, and finally the basic C again. Try this on your ear.

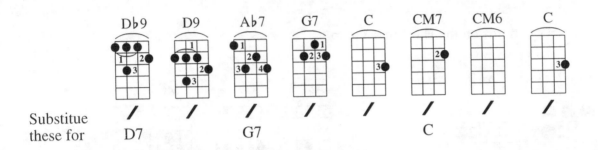

Notice that we followed a one-two, one-two-three-four Hawaiian Vamp rhythm. Only difference is that we changed chords on every beat via jazz basics.

Although I used the Db9, D9, Ab7, G7, C, CM7, C6, and C run, you may use any other combinations. For example, instead of using the Ab7, you may use Ab9; instead of G7, you could use G9, etc.

How To Pick Hawaiian Vamp Runs

If you play in a Hawaiian music group, you will no doubt be using the Hawaiian Vamp strums (II7-V7-I) quite often. In the absence of a steel guitar which usually plays the Hawaiian Vamp runs, you can be a valuable asset to your group by being able to pick the various licks in the Vamp.

On the top of the next page you will see the familiar Vamp that we discussed in the previous pages. A good way to practice any of the runs on the page is to have a partner strum the D7, G7, C for the allotted number of beats while you practice running the picking variations. Lacking a partner, use a tape recorder to record your strumming several times. About ten times should give you plenty of "workout". Play back the strumming while you "fill in" with your runs. Remember that the strumming and picking should start and end on the same beats.

The slant lines represent one beat each for strumming purposes. I put the four beat strumming of the "C" chord at the beginning of each row to indicate the end of a stanza in a typical hula number that ends in the "C" chord.

If you're not too up on your music fundamentals (or if you play entirely by "ear"), have someone who is knowledgeable, teach you the rhythm for each of the runs. Where you see a group of three notes bracketed by a "3" (triplet), that means you play the three notes in the time that it takes to play two.

For example, two eighth notes are usually played with a down-and-up movement of the foot in 4/4 time. When you see the "3" bracketing three eighth notes, you would play the three notes in the time that your foot makes the same down-and-up movement.

If you read music, master the runs in the Key of "C" first and then transpose into other popular keys such as "F", "G", "A", "D" and "Bb".

For variety's sake, don't use the same run through an entire song. I listed four of the most popular Vamp runs on the next page. Use your imagination to create others.

Hawaiian Vamp Runs

Here's a colorful Hawaiian Vamp "lick" that you can add to your repetoire of vamps.

On the previous pages we've been strumming four beats at the end of the hula stanza and then moving into the 8-beat Hawaiian Vamp. For this exercise, you are going to "borrow" two beats from the end of the stanza and use them as "pick-up notes" before moving into the Hawaiian Vamp run.

To clarify, look at the previous page on "Hawaiian Vamp Runs". Notice that at the beginning of each row, there is the measure with four beats (indicated by slant lines) which are to be strummed before moving into the Hawaiian Vamp.

For this exercise, instead of strumming those four beats, you will be strumming only two. The other two beats will be used to run your pick-up notes. Also, instead of using the straight two beat quarter notes, we will use two triplets.

For those of you who play by "ear", review the section on triplets discussed just before the page on the "Hawaiian Vamp Runs".

O. K. The top line is the "straight" Hawaiian Vamp formula. The second line shows the pick-up run.

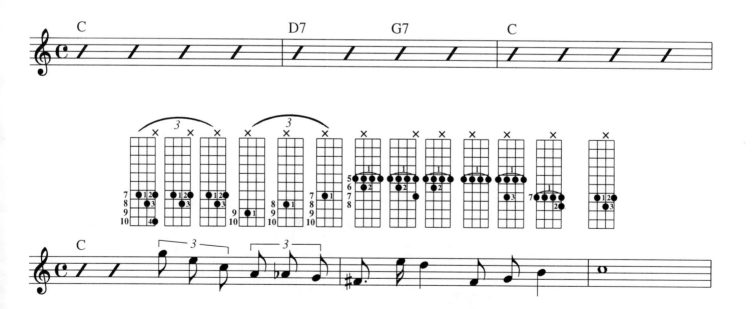

The Rhumba Strum

Latin-American beats on the ukulele can be fun.

The simplest and perhaps the most popular of the Latin-American beats is the basic Rhumba. If you play by "ear", try to figure out the rhythm first and duplicate it either by strumming it or tapping the rhythm on the uke sound box.

If you are familiar with the "Sawtooth Beat" timing system introduced in my booklet "Ukulele By 'Ear', Hawaiian Style", you can figure out the rhythm from the arrowed lines below. If you still can't figure out the rhythm, have someone who can read music tap out the rhythm for you.

Here is the Basic Rhumba Beat

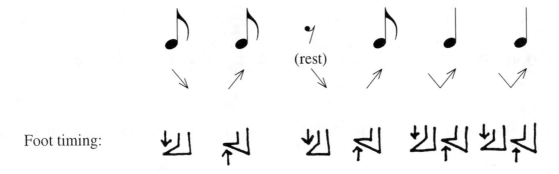

Foot timing:

On a subsequent page you will be applying this Rhumba beat to an excerpt from a song so practice this well before going further.

Holding the "F" chord, do this beat over and over until it becomes second nature to you. Practice shifting back and forth from the "C7th" chord to "F" using the same rhythm.

A good note-reading practice would be to look at each individual note as well as the rest sign as you do the strumming.

On the next page you will find the "animated" pictures of each action that you will be doing as you strum. Follow them closely and practice over and over until it becomes part of your subconscious mind.

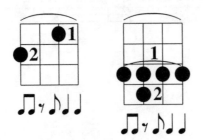

How To Do The Rhumba Strum

Starting position for rhumba rhythm

1. Do downstrum followed by

2. Quick upstrum

(REST)

3. Just drop your hand but don't strum.

4. Follow with upstrum

5. Downstrum

6. Don't strum but just move hand upward

7. Downstrum

8. Don't strum but just move hand upward. Repeat cycle.

If you followed the instructions on the Rhumba Beat, you should have had no trouble strumming the rhythm. On the following page you will be actually working the strumming into an excerpt from a Latin-American melody.

Notice that there are two sections for the first two lines. The top lines indicate the straight melody with basic 4/4 time strumming after picking the melody notes. The bottom two lines show you how to pick and strum the Rhumba Rhythm.

Notice in the top joined section, the first measures are identical. Then the top line second measure shows two half notes while its counterpart in the bottom line shows the Rhumba beat strumming. Even though you see only one note in the lower line, be sure that you strum all four strings. I put the single notes just to remind you about the Rhumba rhythm.

In the third measure, lower line of the first row, notice that you start off with the first half of the Rhumba rhythm but abruptly begin picking the melody. This is because you are the soloist and playing both picking and strumming parts. Notice the same thing happens in the second combination. The first measure shows strumming of the Rhumba beat, but in the second measure, notice that only the first half of the Rhumba Beat cycle is strummed. The second half of that measure is spent picking the melody.

The bottom-most line is a follow-up of the preceding bottom lines. I did not bother to add the straight melody because the melody and rhythm are obvious.

For those who are not used to the pick-strum in this rhythm, follow the strumming patterns exactly as shown in the preliminary exercises. You may use any picking technique that works in with the strumming pattern, be it thumb only, index finger-thumb, or three fingers.

Application Of Rhumba Strumming

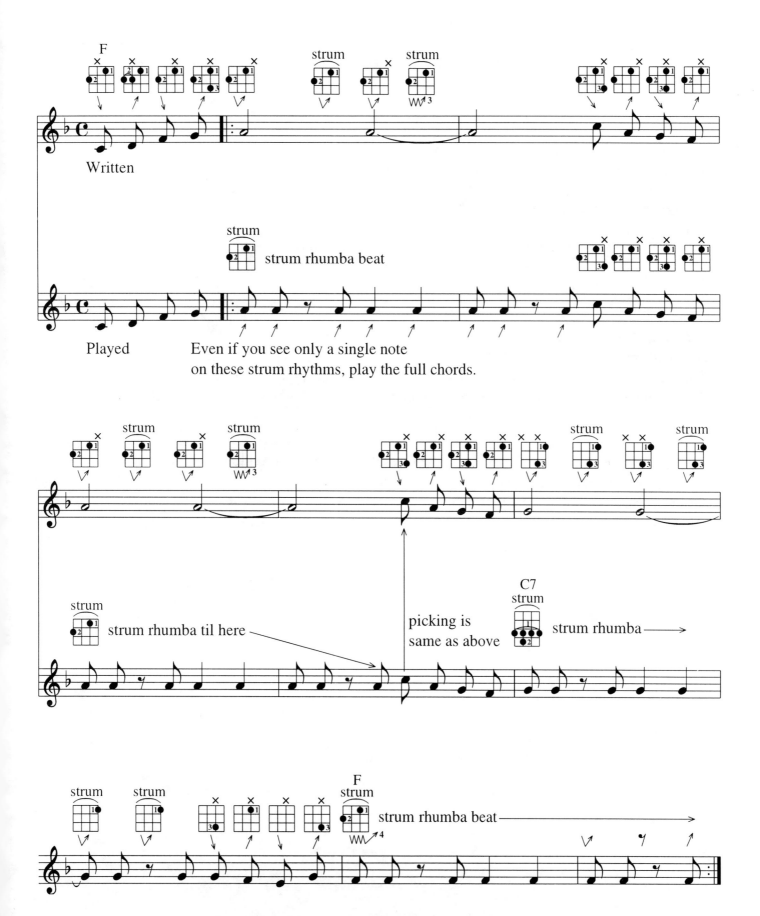

Written

strum rhumba beat

Played   Even if you see only a single note
on these strum rhythms, play the full chords.

strum rhumba til here

picking is
same as above

C7
strum

strum rhumba

F
strum

strum rhumba beat

Don't take this title leterally, but what I mean is that once in a while, when performing before a crowd, you may find that your uke is slightly out of tune. Even experienced players sometimes find that because of the din, it would be impractical to use the standard method of G-C-E-A or "My dog has fleas" tuning.

The most reliable I have found is the "A" tuning check. Instead of having to "memorize" three pitches under the traditional tuning system, you remember only one. If only one string happens to be out of tune, you shouldn't have much trouble, but if more than one are or if you find that your uke is not in tune with other members of your group, you'll find that this "A" tuning check will speed up your "getting on track".

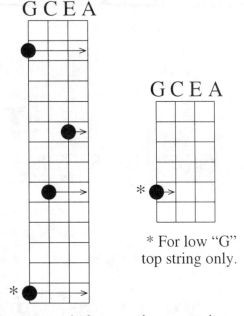

* For low "G"
top string only.

Ask for the "A" note from your fellow players, "memorize" that one pitch, tune the bottom string to that pitch. If you find that your uke is not in tune with other members of your group, you'll find that this "A" tuning check will speed up your "getting on track".

If you use a low "G" for the top string, you would hold the 14th fret to match the open bottom string. However, if your uke has only 12 frets, hold the 5th fret of the top string and match that pitch to the open 3rd string from the bottom. Be sure that this 3rd string ("C" string) has been previously tuned with the bottom "A" string, otherwise, you will compound the "off-tuneness".

Here's a new sound that you may want to work into your ukulele arrangements. Use a very simple major-dominant 7th combination since the emphasis is on the manipulation.

Beat out this rhythm first so that you can "visualize" the timing.

(rest)

If you're not used to this type of rhythm, here's the easier way to do it. Bear in mind that all quarter notes are picked or strummed with a downstroke or as your timing foot hits the floor. Same thing for the eighth notes that occur on the first half of each beat. This may be a bit confusing but let me see if I can clarify it further for you.

(Remember what I mention in this page is in reference to this "knuckle-knock" strum only. Even if I said above that all quarter notes are picked on the downbeat of the foot, don't interpret this to mean that all quarter notes are picked on the downbeat. It's only for this exercise. Let's go on.)

Follow the notes, foot diagrams, and the up or downstrum symbols shown below. Follow them exactly at the beginning. This will make explaining easier.

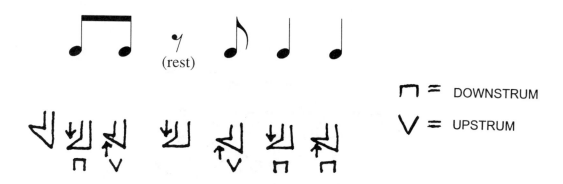

(rest)

⊓ = DOWNSTRUM

V = UPSTRUM

How was it? Now getting to the nitty gritty, notice that here is what you did: You did a down and up strum to take care of the first beat, rested on the next downbeat of the foot and then you made a quick upstrum before coming down twice on the remaining quarter notes.

Remember, even if the single notes are shown here you are strumming across all four strings. The notes are merely to show you the rhythm. Work this pattern over several times until you can "sense" the repetitive rhythm.

Once you are able to strum this rhythm smoothly, you are to substitute a "knuckle knock" against the ukulele fingerboard in place of the "rest". Fold in your last three fingers as shown to do the knock. Use the knuckles closest to the fingernails and tap them gently against the fingerboard. Immediately go to the upstrum of the following eighth note and quickly to the downstrum of the quarter note beat.

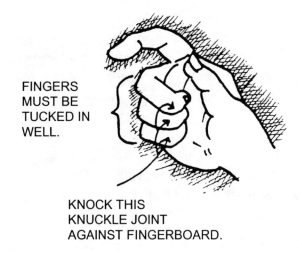

FINGERS
MUST BE
TUCKED IN
WELL.

KNOCK THIS
KNUCKLE JOINT
AGAINST FINGERBOARD.

After you can play the basic knuckle-knock smoothly, you can add a bit of showmanship by knocking on the area between the bridge and the sound hole but above the stringed area. This will produce a hollower and more resonant sound than the flat section of the fingerboard.

BOTTOM OF UKE

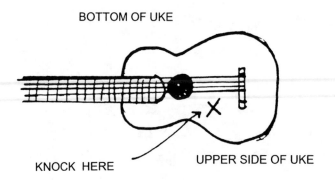

KNOCK HERE

UPPER SIDE OF UKE

Thumb-Knocking For Bongo Effects

Here's a novelty effect you can work into your Latin-American or exotic minor moods rhythm pieces!

First you'll learn the "bongo" effect on the uke sound box. Then we'll add in the strumming part later.

Hold your uke in the regular playing position. If you look at the illustration below, the spot marked "X" on the uke sound box is on the top part of the uke and above the sound hole as you hold the uke with fingerboard to the left of you, and the sound box to your right. (I drew it upside down so that the picture fits your orientation as you hold the uke and look downward). When hitting the box for the "Bongo Knock", use the left side of the thumb tip, lateral to the thumbnail. Follow the illustrations below:

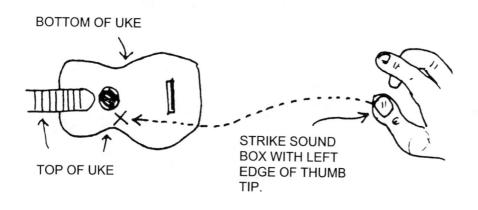

BOTTOM OF UKE

TOP OF UKE

STRIKE SOUND BOX WITH LEFT EDGE OF THUMB TIP.

PRELIMINARY EXERCISE:

STARTING POSTION

1. ROTATE YOUR WRIST TOWARD YOU AS IN FIG. 1 NOTICE THE MOMENTUM POSSIBLE AS THE THUMB ROTATES TOWARD YOU.

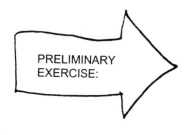

FIG. 1

2. ROTATE WRIST AWAY FROM YOU FOR SECOND HALF. NOTICE THUMB MOVES AWAY.

FIG. 2

3. THEN ADD YOUR UKE!

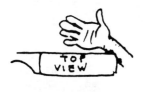

3A. STARTING POSITION

3B. STRIKE THE UKE BOX WITH THUMB.

3C. RETRACT THUMB

Now let's try some basic rhythms that you can practice on:

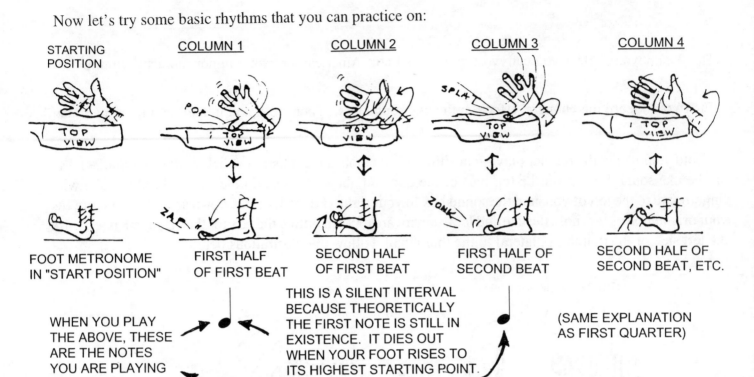

In the exercise above, you hit the box once for each time the foot (timer) hit the floor and rested while it rose. In musical language you played a quarter note each time your foot hit the floor. (4/4 timing).

Now you will practice "hitting" eighth notes timing. For you "ear" players, that means that you will hit the box once when your foot hits the floor and once as it rises up to the starting position. You'll have to tap the box fast in actual timing but start slowly to get the sense of two taps or hits in one beat. I'll try to make it pictorially as clear as possible, but you'll have to follow closely if you're not used to this sort of playing.

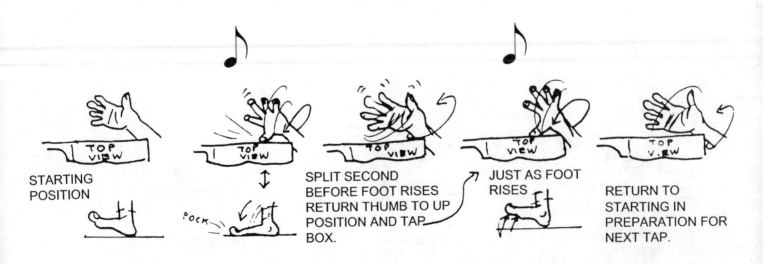

Remember that on this "eighth notes" timing, you are to tap the box twice in one beat. For the "ear" player, you must tap twice in the time that your foot makes a down-and-up timing movement. This means that your arm rotation will have to be twice as fast in order to tap twice (instead of only once as in the single tap in one full beat).

To further clarify, follow this rhythm in your head. I put the hyphen (-) marks to indicate that anything within a pair of them is one full beat.

1. tum-tum-tum-tum   This means that for every beat (or "tum") you thumb knock once. For each
   1   2   3   4   "tum", your foot has made a full down-and-up timing movement. Now try
          some other rhythms.

2. tum-tum-ta ta-tum   This means that the first, second, and fourth beats are single thumb knocks,
   1   2   3   4   but the third beat requires two fast ones (ta ta).

3. ta ta-tum-ta ta-tum   Double knocks on the first and third beats and single ones on the second and
   1   2   3   4   fourth beats.

Got the idea? If so, you can see how you can vary the rhythms to your own taste. This is where your creativity comes into the picture.

O. K. Now that you've got the idea of single and double thumb knocking, let's further refine your thumb knocking techniques.

Study the illustration here. Notice there are two spots marked on the uke sound box. One is close to and abofe the sound hole (marked "X") and the other closer to the bridge (marked "Y").

For your first exercise, thumb knock Spot "Y". Notice that it has a deeper resonant sound as compared to Spot "X". (Knock Spot "X" and compare.)

This difference in sound is what you will use in creating your bongo effects.

Follow the "tum" and "ta ta" business we just talked about by thumb knocking the two spots as shown.

Pattern 1:   Start by knocking Spot "Y" on the first beat, Spot "X" on the second beat, back to Spot "Y" on the third beat, and end with Spot "X" on the last beat. Repeat this over and over until you feel comfortable with the rotative movement of the forearm and the sliding back-and-forth rhythm.

Pattern 2:   Start by knocking Spot "Y" on the first beat, Spot "X" on the second beat, two fast knocks at Spot "Y" on the third beat, and a single knock at Spot "X" on the last beat.

Pattern 3:   Start with double knocks at Spot "Y" on the first beat, a single knock at Spot "X" on the second beat, a double knock again on the third beat at Spot "Y", and ending with a single knock at Spot "X" on the final beat.

So there you have it--the nitty gritty basics of "thumb bongo effects"! Keep practicing the timing over and over until the rhythms and the knocking, plus the arm sliding becomes second nature to you. Experiment with ways of preventing the uke from sliding out from under your arm as you do the movements from Spot "Y" to Spot "X", vice-versa.

When you feel comfortable with the mechanics, go on to the next section on how to add the strings to your knocking.

Thumb Knock With Strumming

Starting position

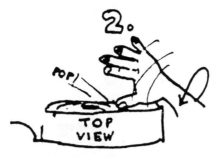

Thumb-knock at spot "Y" (strings omitted to show thumb action.)

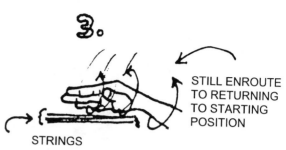

As thumb begins to rotate back to the starting position, keep fingers close to string tops. (uke box omitted above to show hand and strings relation ship.)

Same as step 4 except strum strings closer to sound hole area.

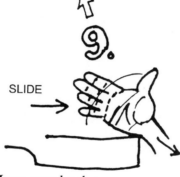

Move arm back to spot "Y" area in preparation for thumb knock at spot "Y" again.

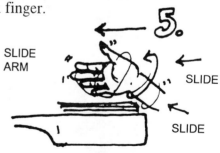

As the thumb moves up and the fingers rotate toward you, skim over all four strings with the fingers or with the index finger.

Same instructions as step 3. keep fingers close to strings.

Tap spot "X" with thumb rotating toward you.

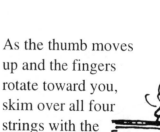

As your fingers clear the strings and move to complete the rotation, slide your arm slightly toward the uke sound hole. This will position the thumb to knock spot "X" above the sound hole.

Maracas Effect

PUT IN SMALL ITEMS
THAT RATTLE.

FIG. 1

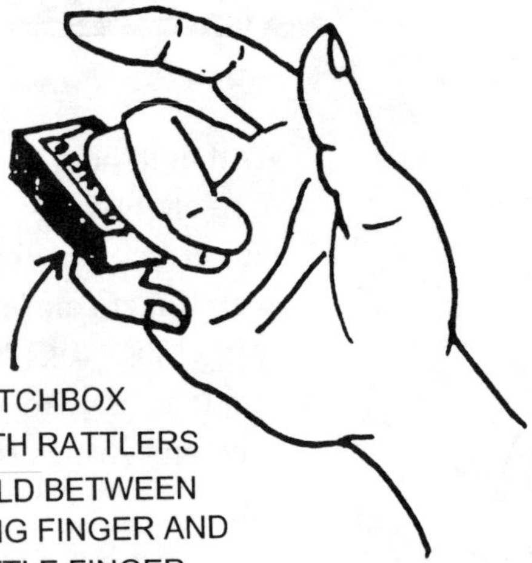

MATCHBOX
WITH RATTLERS
HELD BETWEEN
RING FINGER AND
LITTLE FINGER.

FIG. 2

To create the maracas effect, especially when playing Latin-American songs, get a matchbox about 2" wide and about 1 3/8" wide (See Fig. 1 above), open the drawer and put in a few wooden matchsticks or, if not available, any kind of small gravel or beads that will give you a good rattling sound. Hold it in the position shown in fig. 2, making sure that your index finger and thumb are free to do the picking or strumming. Then just play as you usually do and you'll be pleasantly surprised at the colorful effect. It will add "fullness" to ukes that are playing without accompaniment by other instruments.

Be careful you don't scrape the matchbox against the ukulele for the hardness of the matchbox may mar your wood finish on your uke.

Ukulele Electronics

If you like to tinker with special effects electronically, you'll need an amplifier, a microphone or a ukulele amplifier pick-up device (or both, if you wish), and a double-well tape recording deck or recorder with playback capability.

If you are going to merely play for own enjoyment, the wattage or power of your amplifier doesn't have to be more than 15 watts or so. But if you occasionally play for a group or large socials, get at least a 30-watter.

I play mostly for my own enjoyment but periodically play for parties so I use a Yamaha JX-20 amplifier that puts out 30 watts. I'm no artist but here's a rough sketch of my "box" just to give you an idea.

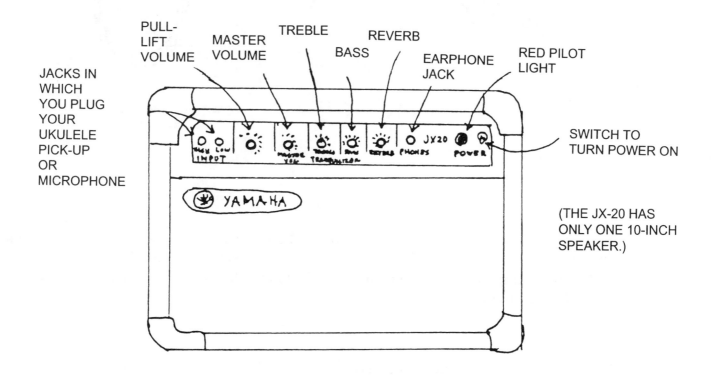

I noticed several years ago that certain mid-priced amplifiers used to have provisions for both "tremelo" and "reverb". I remember building a *Heathkit* amplifier many years ago. Today you'll find "reverb" (which gives a deep chamber echo effect) on the slightly higher priced amplifiers. I'd say, if you were to ask, buy one with a reverb because you can always turn the reverb off when you want to play "plain". At least you'll have the option of one additional feature in your amplifier.

For a ukulele "pick-up" -- the device that feeds the ukulele sound into the amplifier and whose electrical cord plugs into the "input" jack of the amplifier--I have used the "De Armond" brand (which has a volume control) for many years, for want of something more convenient...though I'm not especially thrilled with the fact that after a period of use, it (De Armond) becomes intermittent.

If your amplifier has a healthy output (50 watts plus), you might want to experiment with an omni-directional or uni-directional microphone to amplify your uke output. I like the uni-directional microphone (battery powered) best since it does not pick up as many stray sounds as the omni-directional mike.

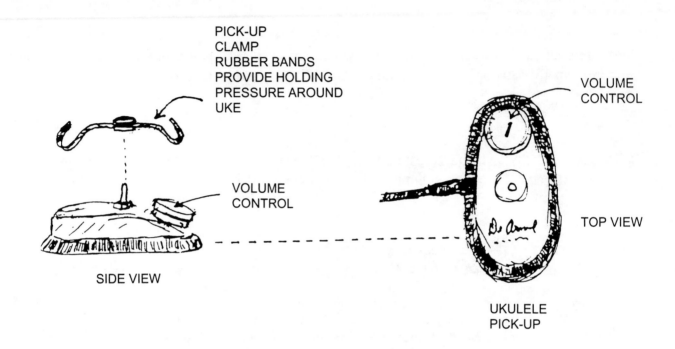

PICK-UP
CLAMP
RUBBER BANDS
PROVIDE HOLDING
PRESSURE AROUND
UKE

VOLUME
CONTROL

VOLUME
CONTROL

SIDE VIEW

TOP VIEW

UKULELE
PICK-UP

It's best to try microphones through your amplifier before playing for a large group. Be certain you're getting enough volume through the amplifier. If you get one that really booms, you've got a "winner". A good microphone will afford you more freedom. The pick-up chord on the ukulele can stifle you playing to a limited extent.

A useful item to have is a tape recorder to record one part of your uke playing, play it back while you play the second part (usually strumming "accomps").

However, don't make the mistake I made. In my naivete, I thought I could take two inexpensive portable tape recorder first, then play back that initial solo while accompanying myself. I then recorded both parts on the second tape recording--the result was terrible. Because of the poor matching (which I later discovered), the sound was grossly distorted.

You can get good multiple recordings by investing in a good double well tape recorder and playback deck. For weekend ukers, a professional deck is not necessary. The currently popular "karaoke" types may be adequate unless you are an audiophile and are very discriminating in sound. In case you are wondering what a "well" is, it's the receptacle for an audio cassette tape. The usual portable tape recorder or playback machine has only one, the kind I'm talking about has two.

With the double-well you can put a recorded tape in one well and a blank tape in the other, to either dub in your uke accompaniment, or to merely duplicate the original recording.

If you plan to buy a double-well, here are some suggestions:

1. Buy a "pure" double-well! If there are features like AM-FM radio on the recorder, pass it up for one that is strictly a recorder-playback. In your enthusiasm, don't buy any ol' double-well you see. Buy one that was built for recording and dubbing. Don't pay for radio.

2. Make doubly sure that the double-well recorder you buy has provision for dubbing--namely a microphone receptacle (usually a phone jack input marked "mic"). Otherwise, you'll be able to record only one part at a time and not accompany yourself--which is really your purpose in the first place for buying the recorder.

3. Insist on hearing how the recorder performs. If possible, take along two blank audio cassette tapes (some firms do not provide these.)Take the time to record on one and dub on the second tape. Take your uke along, too, because straight talking alone will not necessarily give you the quality indication for uke sounds.

I have tried some double welled recorders that sounded okay on voice but a sort of wavering, tinny sound when ukulele music was recorded. So be sure to test and ask a lot of questions (think of them ahead and jot them down!) because once you buy and discover any undesireable characteristic (not necessarily flaws), you may find yourself stuck with an unsatisfactory product.

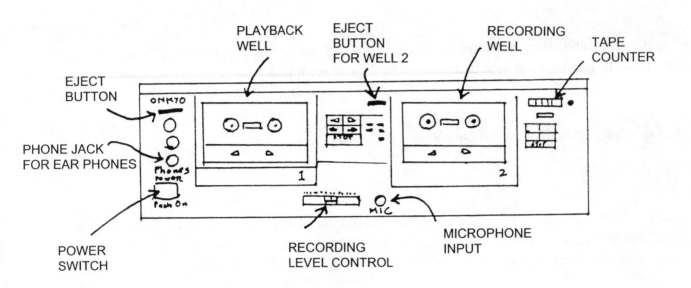

Above is a very rough sketch of my tape deck just to point out some of the essential features you should have on your double-well recorder.

Remember there's a difference between a tape "deck" and a complete recorder that has a built-in play-back amplifier and speaker. If you buy only a tape recorder "deck", you will be able to record your playing by plugging in a microphone to the deck but you won't be able to hear the playback since a "deck" is usually not provided with an amplifier and loudspeaker. A deck must be hooked up to an existing amplifier-speaker system.

You can get around this--if you don't happen to have an amplifier playback unit handy--by plugging in a set of earphones into your deck. Then you can hear everything that's going into the deck while recording as well as when you play it back.

Buying only a deck if you don't have any amplifier-loudspeaker system may seem illogical to some, but the big advantage of the tape recorder deck is that dollar-for-dollar you are paying for better recording quality as compared to a tape recorder that is a complete unit but has poorer sound quality and frills (such as Am-Fm radio) you don't necessarily need.

"Two-On-One Novelty"

To add humor and enhance entertainment value to your performance at your next party, announce that you can make anyone an "instant" ukulele player.

Then call up anyone who is willing and instruct him or her to stand behind you as you sit on a chair or stool. Tell your volunteer to use his/her index finger to stroke downward only while counting aloud "1-2-3-4" in time to the down strums.

While that is being done, you pick a simple song with your right hand while holding the chords with your left hand. Picking only single string melodies will not sound harmonious--you must be holding chords with your left as you pick with your right (vice-versa if you pick left-handed). Leave room at the center of your fingerboard for your volunteer to strum.

Using Your Tape Recorder To Improvise

Improvising by "ear" is fun when you understand the basic principles. Knowledge of chord analysis and structure are important but if you're a week-end player, you may not want to be too "intellectual" in your approach to improvising (also known as "ad libbing" in musical circles).

"Improvising" means to change the melody of a song depending on the individual taste of the player. Some improvisations stick pretty close to the original melody of a song usually filling in extra notes on the notes that are sustained. The opposite extreme is when the ad lib is so "far out" that the basic melody is unrecognizable.

The techniques of improvisation are beyond the scope of this book. But one creative way you can experiment with ad libbing is to record a straight melody on your tape recorder several times. You repeat the tune enough times so you won't have to rewind the recorder as often. Then as you are listening to the playback, you superimpose your improvised version of the song.

By having the "straight" melody as a background, you'll know whether your improvised version "fits" the basic melody or not: Meaning, for example, if there is sustained note in the melody and you opt to do a short melodic "run" instead of sustaining the same note, your "run" must equal the value of that sustained note, not less, not more.

When improvising, it's best to work closely around the melody so you will know where you are in the song. Later as you get better, you may want to get away from the melody and run scales around the chords.

This is really an oversimplified description of improvising because a performer is limited only by his imagination! For your purpose, the two-part simultaneous playing, using the basic melody and working around it with short phrases should give your creativity a good "workout".

Adapting To Different Picking Methods

Whether you use the thumb alone, thumb and index, thumb and two fingers (index and middle fingers), reinforced index finger ala guitar pick style, or what-have-you, it's a good idea (and fun) to try modes which are unfamiliar to you.

Certain songs that require speed can be more efficiently played by one method than another. Let's use "Hawaiian War Chant" to discuss the different possibilities:

Play the excerpt to the song shown on the next page, using your thumb and index finger skill. Under this method, you would use the index finger to pick the bottom two strings and the thumb to pick the top two strings in a downward motion. If you are not familiar with this method, work on it and enjoy the muscle reeducation to give you greater versatility.

Then you can try the thumb method using all down movements as you pick "Hawaiian War Chant". Use the fleshy part of the thumb for this.

If you keep your thumbnail slightly long for uke purposes, you are probably familiar with the thumbnail method using it either in all down movements OR down-and-up movements like a guitar pick. There are two basic methods--one with the thumb extended straight and facing toward the ukulele and the other with the thumb bent and "claw-like". Wrist action is important in both methods as there is a tendency to hold the arm too rigidly.

A variation to the thumb and index picking technique is to use the thumb and index finger alternately regardless of which string contains the melody note. Under this method the thumb and index finger could pick successive notes on the same string. No assignment of strings for thumb and index here.

Reinforced index method: Under this method, the index finger is used like a pick in up-and-down plectum movements. The thumb is braced against the index finger at the junction of the first and second tarsal joints of the index finger.

Try all of the above just for exposure. Work them into your own uke arrangements to add "color" and showmanship.

The "Finger Roll Picking (Plucking)"

The "finger roll plucking" adds showmanship as well as pleasant sound variety to your style. We'll go step-by-step using this phrase:

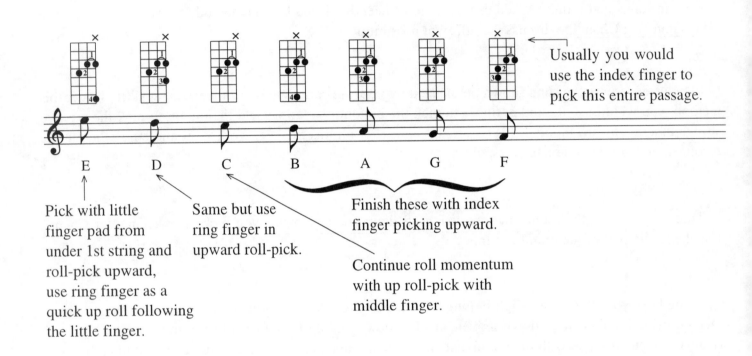

Usually you would use the index finger to pick this entire passage.

E   D   C   B   A   G   F

Pick with little finger pad from under 1st string and roll-pick upward, use ring finger as a quick up roll following the little finger.

Same but use ring finger in upward roll-pick.

Continue roll momentum with up roll-pick with middle finger.

Finish these with index finger picking upward.

DIRECTION OF ROLL-PICK.

KEEP LITTLE AND RING FINGERS CLOSE; HOWEVER, LITTLE FINGER PICKS FIRST FOLLOWED CLOSELY BY RING FINGER.

How To Do The "Slur"

Here's a "flashy" lick you can add to your repertoire.

Pick the x'ed strings only.

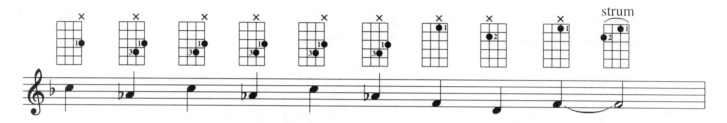

For this preliminary overly simplified exercise, notice that the third finger is used for the second string. This is to prepare you for the "slur".

Now add the extra note.

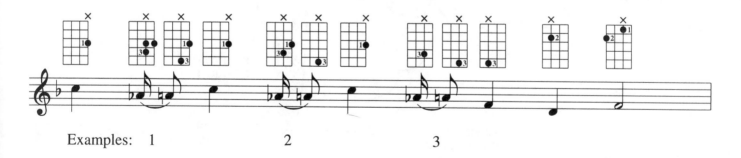

Examples: 1   2   3

This may feel kind of stiff, but main thing is the sliding or "slurring" 3rd (ring) finger from 2nd to 3rd fret.

Now play the regular speed.

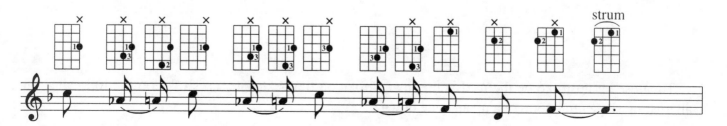

Picking "Hawaiian War Chant"

First, pick the "X'ed" strings to learn the melody. If you don't know the melody, spend the time to learn it well.

Then when you can play "the chant" pretty well, follow the picking styles one at a time as described on the previous page entitled "adapting to different picking methods".

When you get to the "reinforced index finger" method, first follow the uke diagrams as shown on the next page. Start the first note with a down stroke of the reinforced index finger. The thumb is held firm but not rigidly against the index finger.

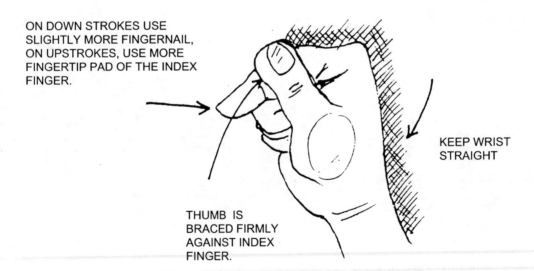

ON DOWN STROKES USE SLIGHTLY MORE FINGERNAIL, ON UPSTROKES, USE MORE FINGERTIP PAD OF THE INDEX FINGER.

KEEP WRIST STRAIGHT

THUMB IS BRACED FIRMLY AGAINST INDEX FINGER.

Then use an upstroke on the next note, down stroke on the next note, up stroke on the following, etc., alternating sequential notes one up and one down.

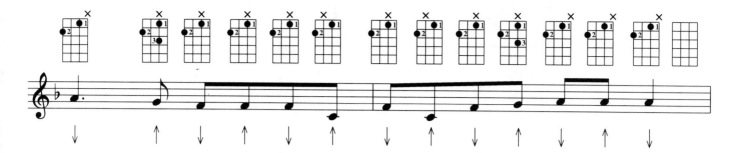

The arrows tell you whether you pluck the strings down or up. Start slowly and experiment on the best angles for your index finger to pluck up and down, as everyone's hands are structured differently.

Take time out now and notice the length of your fingers. If the three fingers in the middle of your hand are nearly equal in length, you are most likely more manually dexterous than a person with uneven lengths. However, practice can overcome any structural disadvantage.

Once you have gone through the fingering at the top of this page, try this variation:

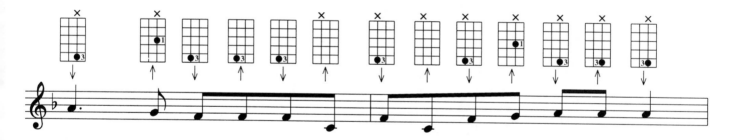

You'll notice that the second version is easier, speedwise. That's because you used only two strings whereas in the top-of-the-page version, you had to use three. The up-and-down continuous picking also gave you no wasted motion if compared to the "only downstroke" or "only upstroke" picking styles.

To give you a good insight into how you can streamline your picking, go through the fingering of "The Hawaiian War Chant" on the next page first and start slowly but, once you can play it pretty well, pick up the speed until you are playing it to your maximum without sacrificing proper timing and clearness of each string. Be sure to use all styles of picking (thumb-index, thumb-index-middle, thumbs only, and the reinforced index).

Hawaiian War Chant

(Excerpt)

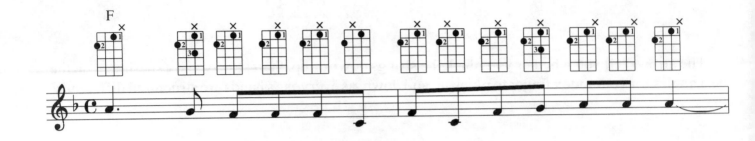

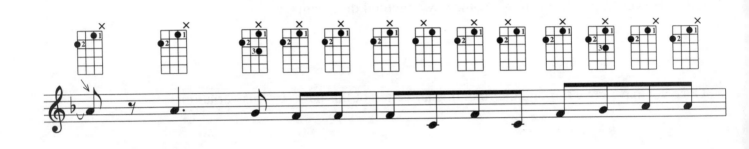

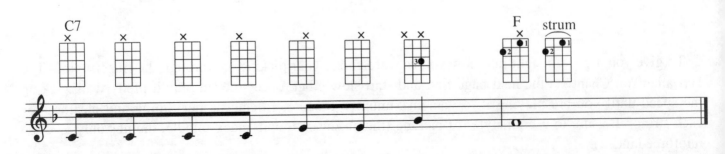

O.K. Now that you got your feet wet with basic speed picking, play this two-string version of the same song.

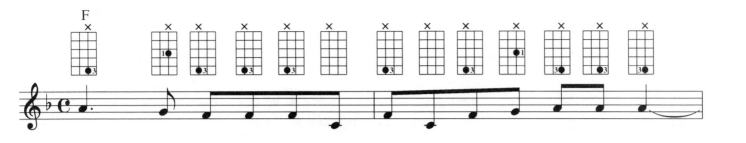

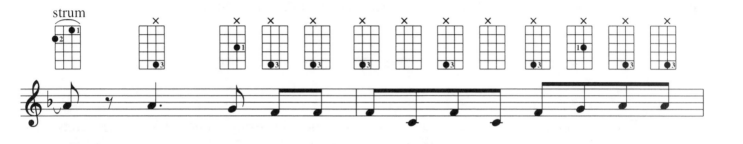

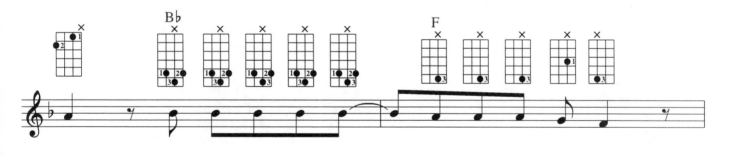

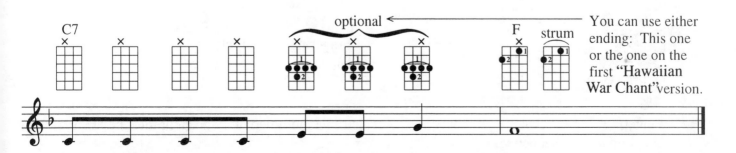

You can use either ending: This one or the one on the first "Hawaiian War Chant" version.

How To Run Scales

The best way to develop your finger dexterity is to practice scale runs. Even if you play by "ear", you should be able to figure out the following patterns in running scales.

The diagram labeled "fingering" shows you which finger to use for each note. The "1" means your index finger, "2" is your middle finger, "3" is your ring finger, and "4" is your little finger.

The diagram next to the corresponding "fingering" diagram is the "picking sequence" diagram. The numbers tell you the order in which you pick the respective "do-re-mi" scales.

Be sure you don't get confused on the numbers. Each diagram has a different purpose!

The "0" in the "fingering" diagram means you merely pick the string without holding any frets. The counterpart on the "picking sequence" diagram is the number "1" which means you pick that open string first.

Do the following runs. Memorize both the fingering patterns as well as the name of the key for each run you make.

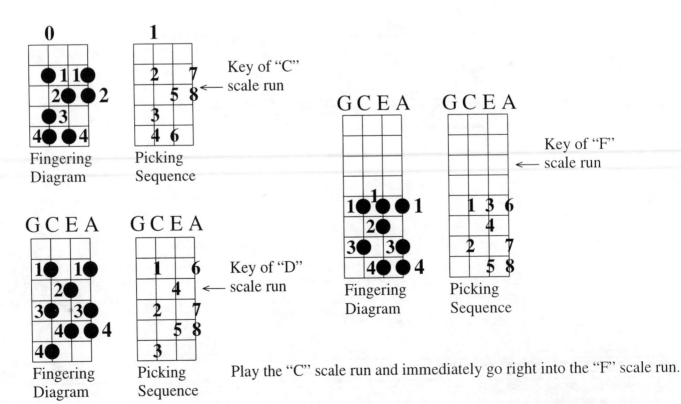

Here's a "do-re-mi" scale warm-up you can do in 12 keys. Practice each scale separately first. Then play all 12 in their proper order for your daily warm-up. A few practice sessions of this can literally make your fingers "fly all over the fingerboard".

Notice very carefully that the numbers in each diagram tell you the <u>order or sequence</u> of the strings to pick, <u>not</u> the fingering! (see previous page for details.)

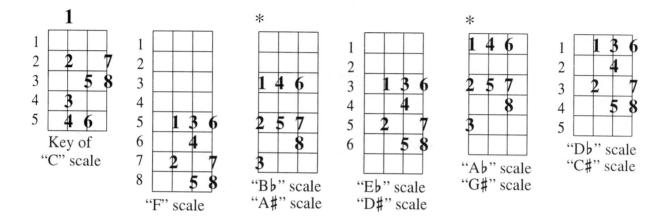

(* Scales that start on the top string will sound one octave higher unless you use a low "G" string.)

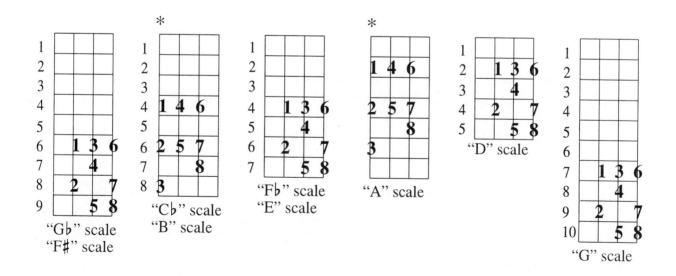

Expanding Your Chord
"Savvy"

Listed on the next 13 pages are the most complete basic chord charts. There are as many as seven different ways to hold a fundamental or semi-advanced chord. As you become more familiar with the chord structures, you will no doubt be able to add more.

It is best to stick with the basic major, dominant seventh, minor, diminished, and augmented chords to do your basic uke arrangements at first. Then if the nature of the song lends itself to more colorful chords, then by all means begin to add to your creativity with particles of 11th, 13th, and lowered and raised fifths, etc. But there is such a thing as overdoing fancy chords. Uppermost and "hearable" should be the basic melody when ad-libbed or straight. The chords should be used essentially to enhance or add "color" to that melody.

Despite having a limited "handicap" of only four strings, the ukulele has the capability of some interesting chord progressions. However, unless the "bogus" chords are used sparingly and in the most appropriate passages, the beauty of the arrangement is rendered monotonous with an overabundance of "offbeat" chords.

Don't try to "force memorize" the advanced chords on the following pages. Use the charts as reference sources. Seek out published sheet music of your favorite songs--the ones that have chord designations also --and study the suggested chords. Often you'll come across some good progressions that you may want to incorporate into your arrangements.

Good luck in expressing your ukulele creativity!

Major Chords

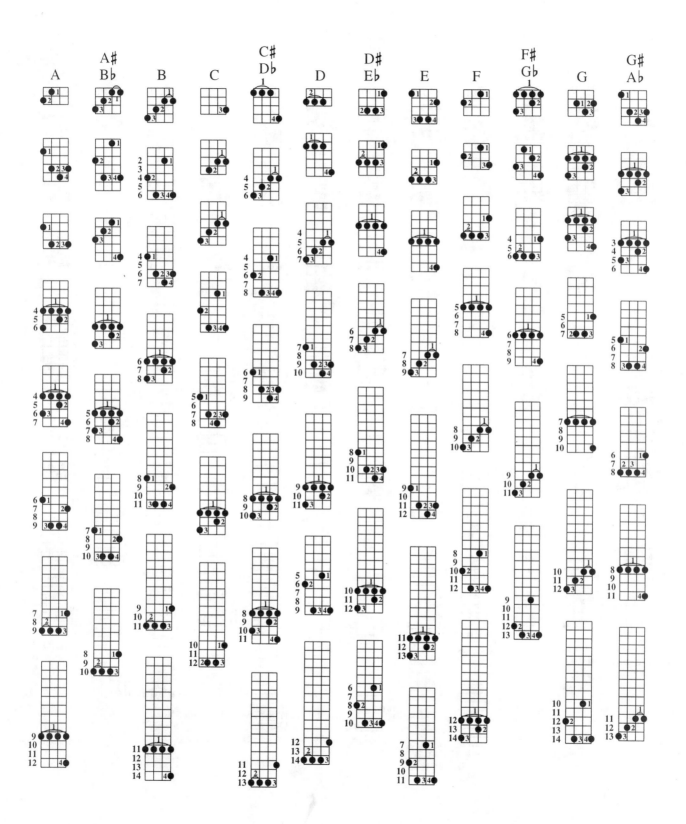

Minor Chords

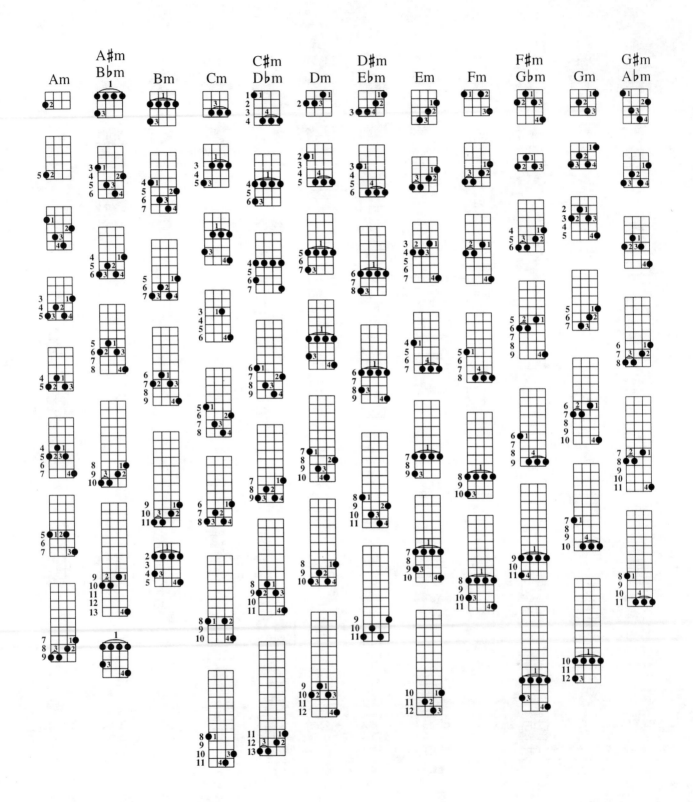

Dominant
Seventh (7th) Chords

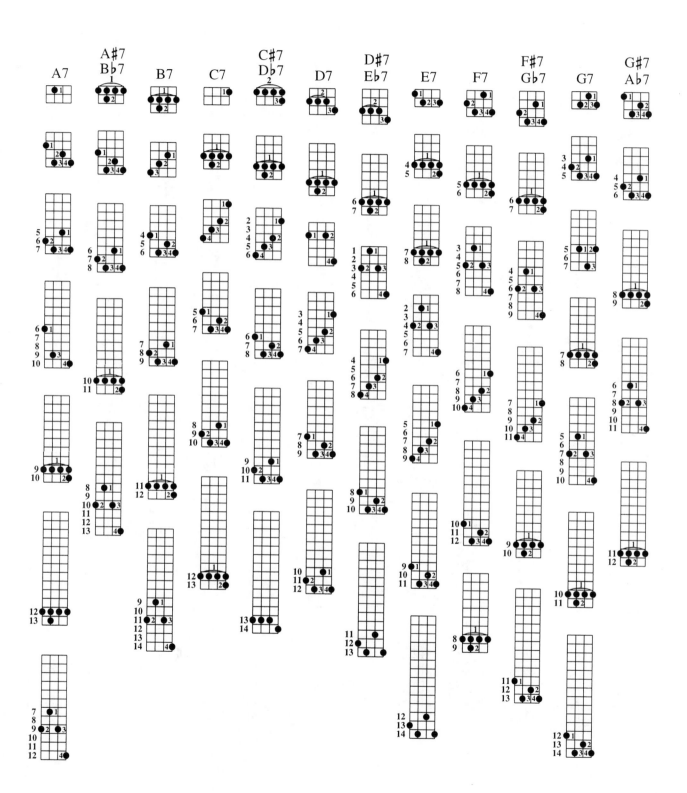

Dominant Seventh Chords
With Lowered Fifth

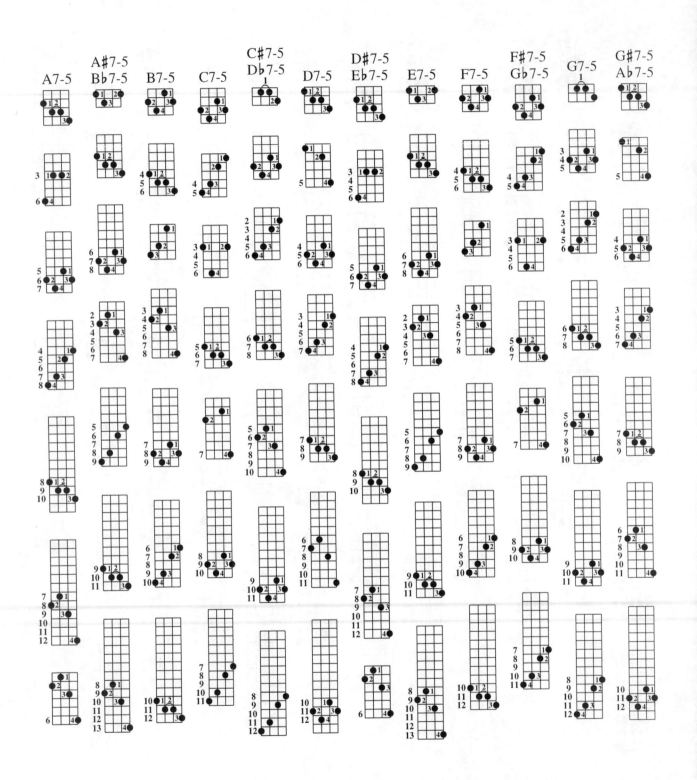

Dominant
Ninth (9th) Chords

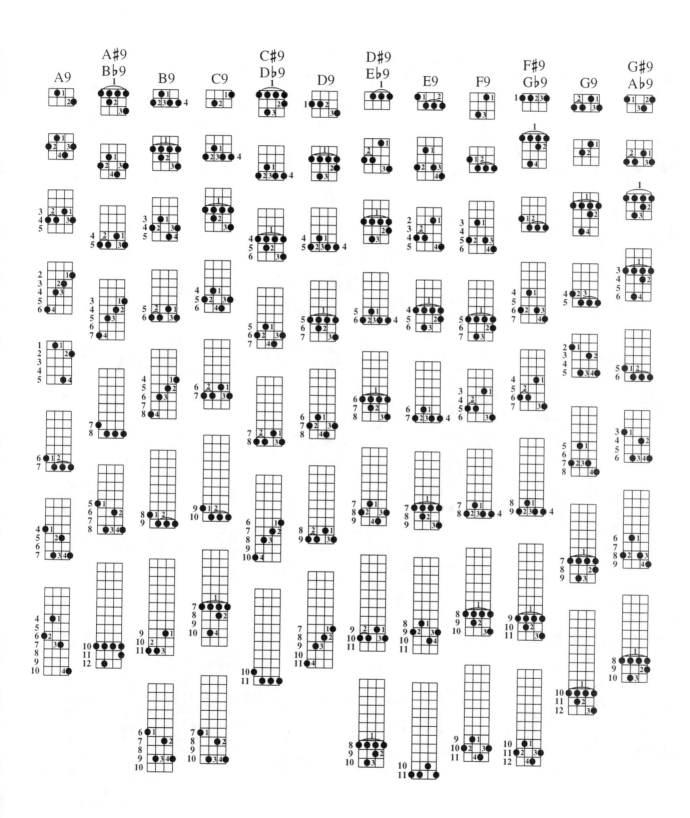

Dominant Seventh Chords
With Raised Fifth

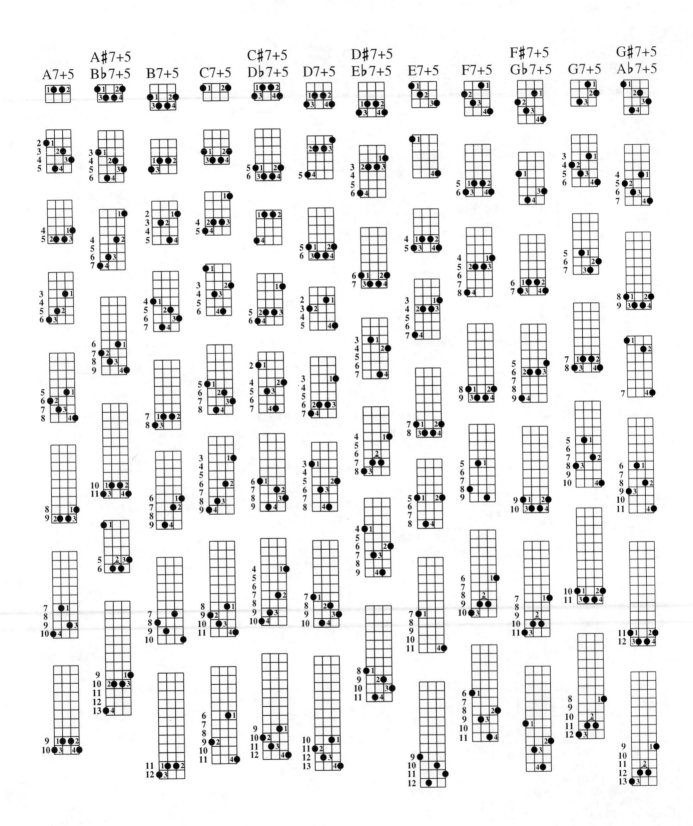

Major Seventh Chords

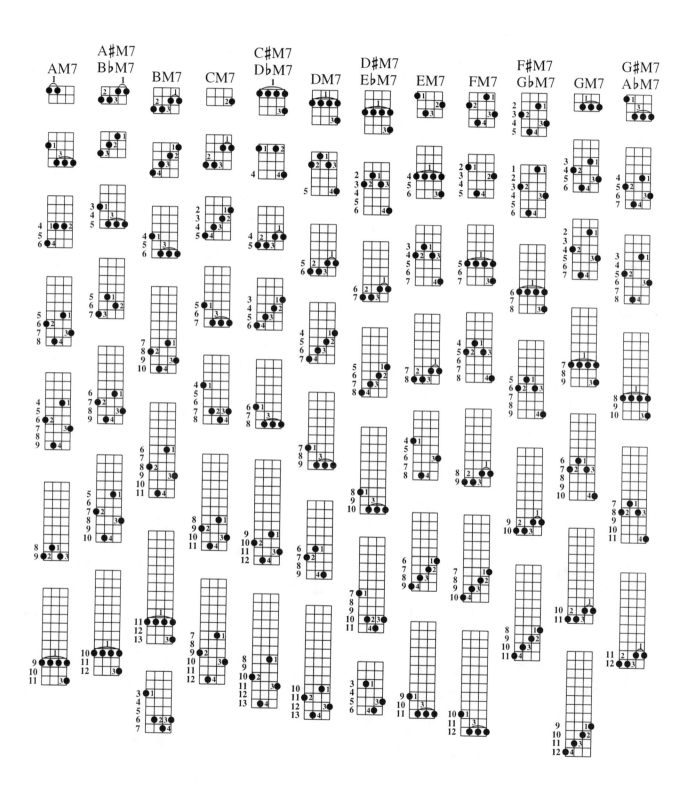

61

Major Sixth Chords

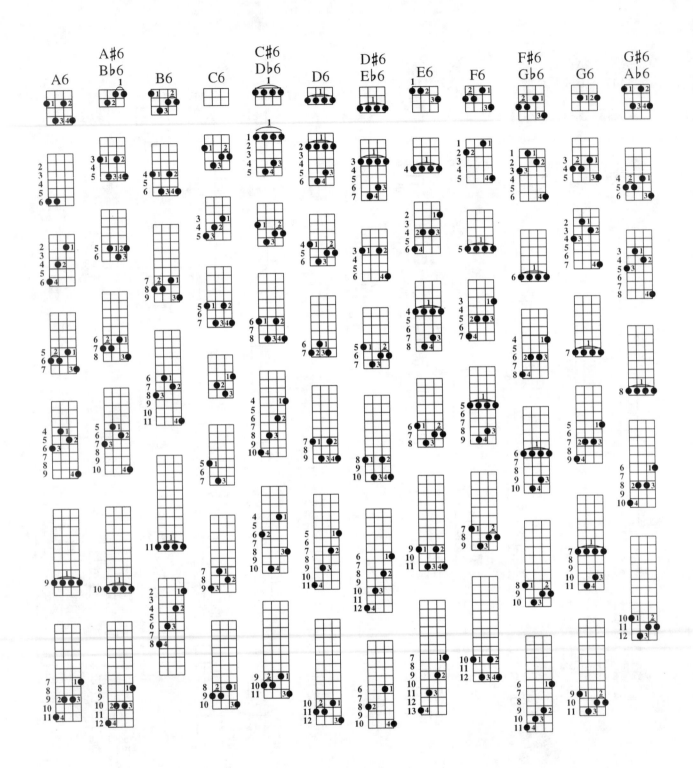

Minor Seventh Chords

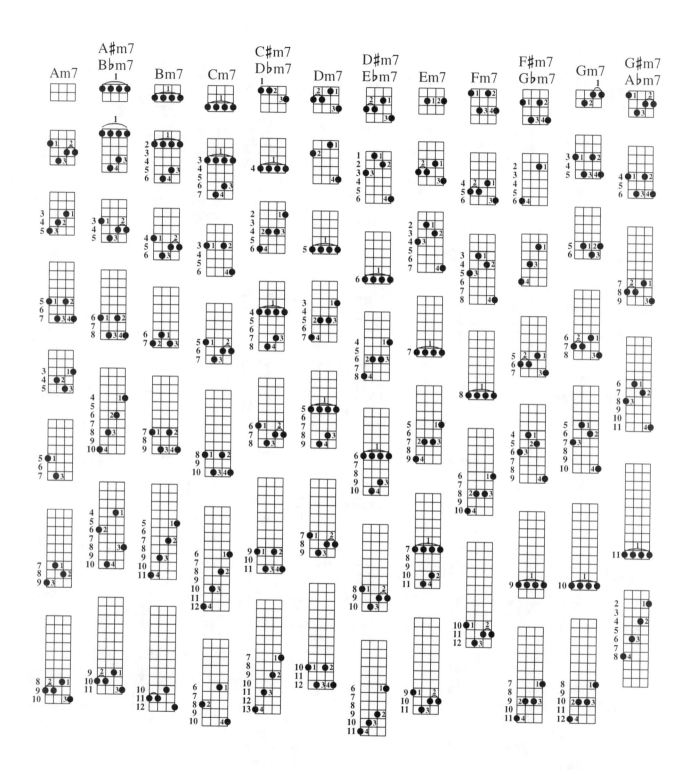

Minor Sixth Chords

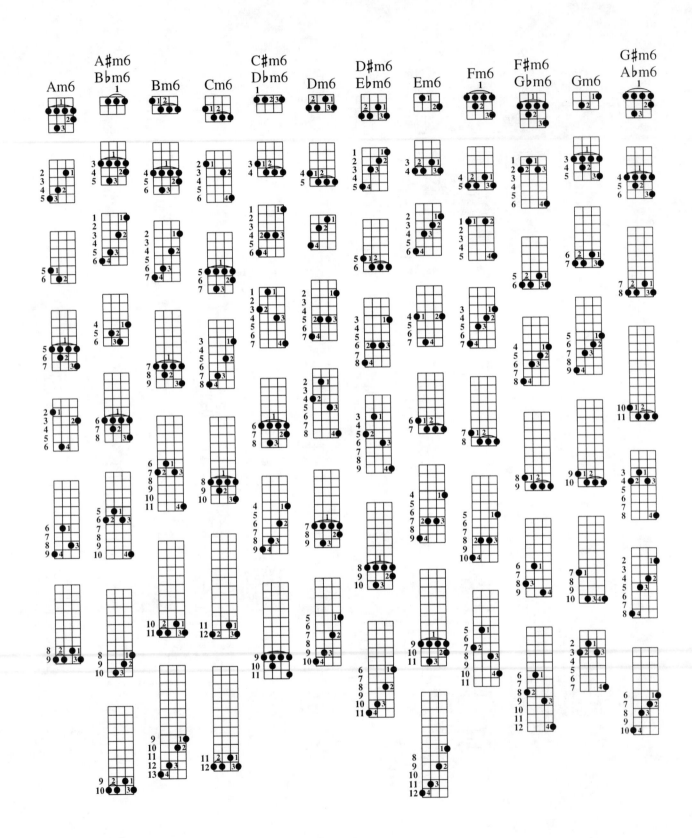

Diminished Seventh Chords

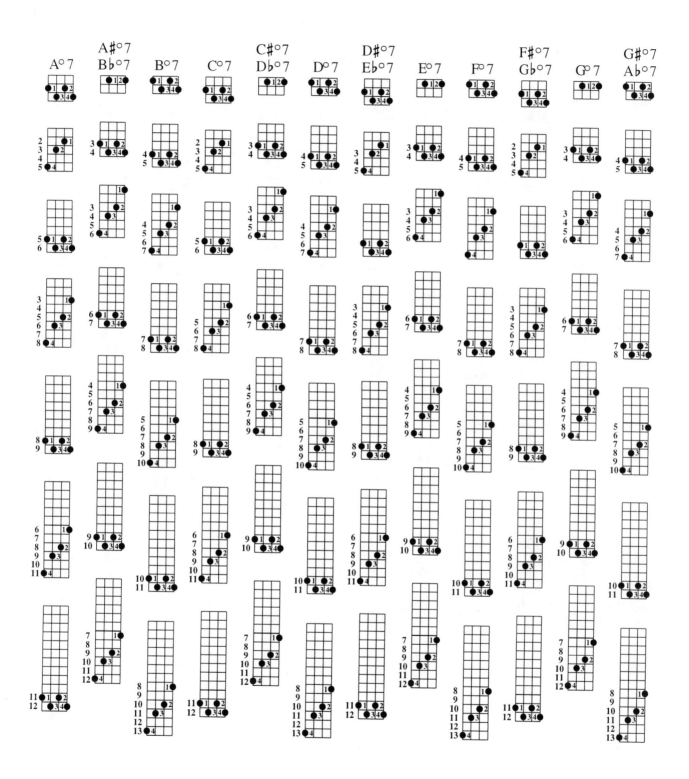

Augmented Chords

+ = "augmented"

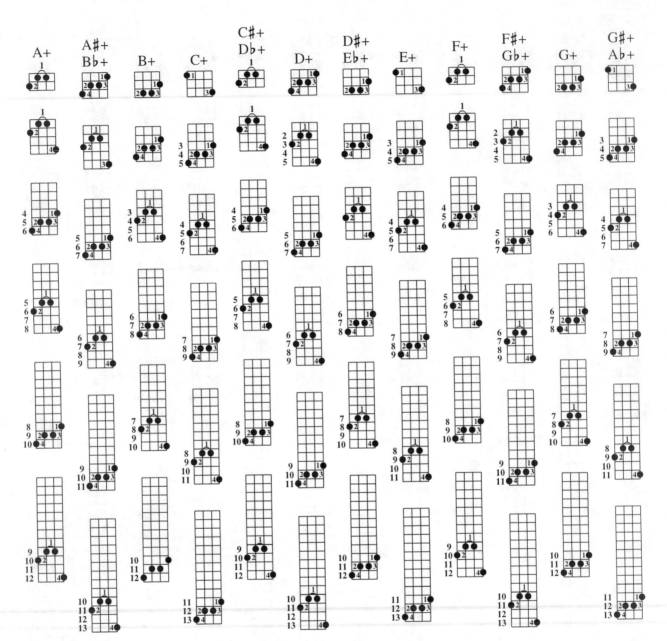

Major Ninth Chords
(With 5th omitted)

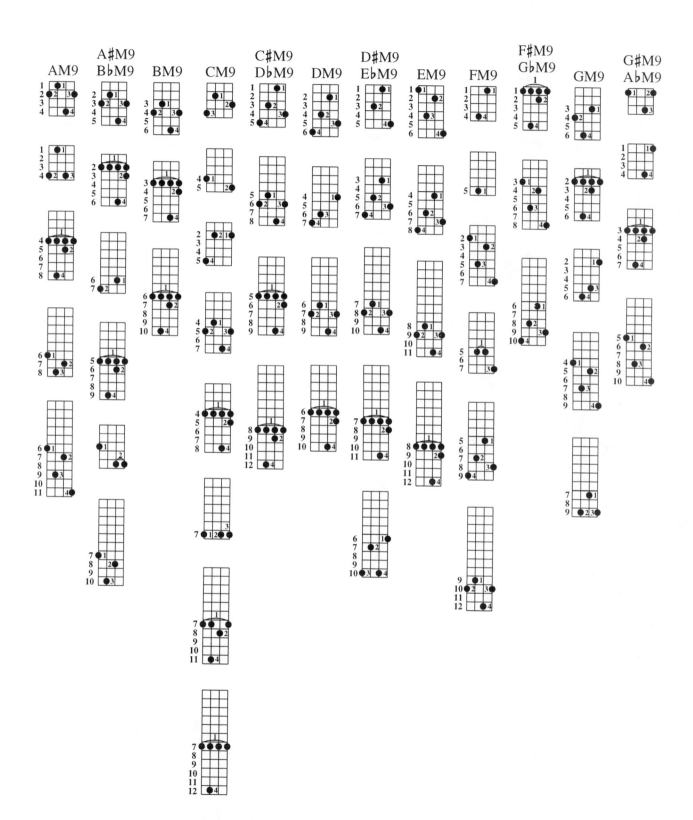